At Issue

| Cell Phones and Driving

Other Books in the At Issue Series:

At Issue

|Cell Phones and Driving

Roman Espejo, Book Editor

GREENHAVEN PRESS
A part of Gale, Cengage Learning

GALE
CENGAGE Learning·

Farmington Hills, Mich • San Francisco • New York • Waterville, Maine
Meriden, Conn • Mason, Ohio • Chicago

Elizabeth Des Chenes, *Director, Content Strategy*
Douglas Dentino, *Manager, New Product*

© 2015 Greenhaven Press, a part of Gale, Cengage Learning.

WCN: 01-100-101

Gale and Greenhaven Press are registered trademarks used herein under license.

For more information, contact:
Greenhaven Press
27500 Drake Rd.
Farmington Hills, MI 48331-3535
Or you can visit our Internet site at gale.cengage.com

For product information and technology assistance, contact us at

Gale Customer Support, 1-800-877-4253
For permission to use material from this text or product, submit all requests online at www.cengage.com/permissions

Further permissions questions can be e-mailed to permissionrequest@cengage.com

Articles in Greenhaven Press anthologies are often edited for length to meet page requirements. In addition, original titles of these works are changed to clearly present the main thesis and to explicitly indicate the author's opinion. Every effort is made to ensure that Greenhaven Press accurately reflects the original intent of the authors. Every effort has been made to trace the owners of copyrighted material.

Cover image © Images.com/Corbis.

LIBRARY OF CONGRESS CATALOGING-IN-PUBLICATION DATA

Cell phones and driving / Roman Espejo, book editor.
    pages cm. -- (At issue)
    Includes bibliographical references and index.
    ISBN 978-0-7377-7155-8 (hardcover : alk. paper) -- ISBN 978-0-7377-7156-5 (pbk. : alk. paper)
    1. Cell phones and traffic accidents. 2. Distracted driving. 3. Traffic safety--United States. I. Espejo, Roman, 1977-
    HE5620.D59C452 2015
    363.12'51--dc23
                                                        2014021950

Printed in the United States of America
1 2 3 4 5 6 7 18 17 16 15 14

Contents

Introduction

Overall, adult cell phone owners send or receive an average of 41.5 texts a day, according to the Pew Research Internet Project. Those between eighteen and twenty-four years old send or receive considerably more—an average of 109.5 texts a day, or about 3,200 text messages a month. And in this age group, 12 percent send or receive an average of two hundred texts or more a day, or six thousand a month. "No group compares to young adults when it comes to text messaging, although several other groups do text on a daily basis at higher-than-average levels,"[1] states Aaron Smith, a senior researcher with the Pew Research Internet Project. "For example, non-whites (African Americans in particular) text more often than whites, and those with lower levels of income and education text more often than those at the higher end of the income and education scale." He adds that the type of mobile device makes a difference in texting habits. "Smartphone owners (mean=52.0, median=20) also send and receive a significantly larger number of texts per day than owners of more basic phones (mean=29.7, median=10)," Smith explains.

Some of this text messaging occurs when people drive, which is a growing and alarming concern across the nation. The National Highway Traffic Safety Administration (NHTSA) estimates that at any given time during the day, 660,000 Americans are using cell phones or other devices behind the wheel. "Many drivers see distracted driving as risky when other drivers do it, but do not recognize how their own driv-

---

1. Aaron Smith, "How Americans Use Text Messaging," Pew Research Internet Project, September 19, 2011. http://www.pewinternet.org/2011/09/19/how-americans-use-text -messaging.

ing deteriorates,"[2] asserts David Strickland, an NHTSA administrator. "I urge all motorists to use common sense and keep their attention focused solely on the task of safely driving."

The apparent disconnect in drivers between knowing the dangers of texting and driving—but still doing it—has prompted greater research into the issue. "It seems clear something powerful is at work, overriding people's knowledge that what they're doing behind the wheel is dangerous,"[3] proposes Leon Neyfakh, a staff reporter at the *Boston Globe*. Neyfakh contends that texting and driving is much more complex than being careless or acting impulsively; instead, technology is fundamentally changing the way people behave. "It's not like the judgment error of drinking too much and deciding to drive home anyway; it's not like neglecting to put on your seat belt," Neyfakh claims. "Our phones have effectively programmed us with new habits, including a powerful urge to pull them out when we're not supposed to," he continues. "That urge—to check our e-mail, to glance at Facebook, to see who just texted us—can be as intense when we're standing in line or at dinner with our families as it is when we're driving a car."

For instance, Neyfakh cites a study in which participants were provided smartphones with software that monitored their use of the devices for six weeks. The results showed that they looked at their smartphones up to sixty times a day, qualifying as habitual behavior. As indicated in diary entries, participants who constantly checked their e-mail or read the news said that they did so out of boredom. Referring to psychologists' understanding of habitual behavior, Neyfakh in-

2. NHTSA, "NHTSA Survey Finds 660,000 Drivers Using Cell Phones or Manipulating Electronic Devices While Driving at Any Given Daylight Moment," United States Department of Transportation, August 2013. http://www.dot.gov/briefing-room/nhtsa-survey-finds-660000-drivers-using-cell-phones-or-manipulating-electronic-devices.
3. Leon Neyfakh, "Why You Can't Stop Checking Your Phone," *Boston Globe*, October 6, 2013. http://www.bostonglobe.com/ideas/2013/10/06/why-you-can-stop-checking-your-phone/rrBJzyBGDAr1Y1EH5JQDcM/story.html.

sists that certain triggers compel people to automatically or involuntarily reach for their phones. "These triggers can be quite basic—the phone ringing or buzzing with a message—and they can come from inside as well as out. One's desire to reach for the phone might be rooted in complex emotions like loneliness and curiosity, for instance,"[4] he observes.

Furthermore, some experts tell the *Boston Globe* that cell phone habits and their triggers do not simply vanish in the driver's seat. "The idea that you can just turn off all those associations when you get into the car—I just don't think it's realistic,"[5] maintains Stephen O'Connor, a psychologist at Western Kentucky University who cowrote a paper on phone use and the incidence of motor vehicle accidents. In fact, Paul Atchley, a psychologist at the University of Kansas, theorizes that the act of driving itself may lower a person's control over such habits because it engages the neural area that governs inhibition. "The part of your brain that would say, 'Don't do this, this is bad for you,' is occupied,"[6] he claims.

The psychological view that people text while driving out of deeply ingrained behaviors presents a conundrum to lawmakers and others seeking to protect the roads. Some suggest, for example, that hands-free technology such as voice activation and in-dash displays can prevent drivers from habitually picking up their phones to send and check messages. In contrast, others argue that hands-free technology does not actually reduce the cognitive distraction of texting or talking on the phone and creates the illusion of safety. *At Issue: Cell Phones and Driving* investigates this emerging problem of driver distraction as well as the available and proposed solutions.

4. Ibid.
5. Quoted in Neyfakh.
6. Quoted in Neyfakh.

1

Cell Phone Use Is Not Linked to Significantly More Accidents

Saurabh Bhargava and Vikram S. Pathania

Saurabh Bhargava is an assistant professor of economics, social and decision sciences at Carnegie Mellon University. Vikram S. Pathania is a fellow in the department of management at the London School of Economics and Political Science.

Recent research confirms the belief that cell phone use while driving increases the risk of an accident—by 4.3 fold, according to an influential paper. However, a unique approach does not support such a causal link. First, even as cellular ownership and call minutes have significantly risen, aggregate crash rates have fallen in the same period. Moreover, a study of drivers' cellular data at the 9 p.m. threshold—when call prices are off-peak—shows that the likelihood of calls increases by 7.2 percent but the risk of crashing does not increase by 4.3 fold. It is possible that some drivers compensate for the dangers of cell phone use with safer driving or substitute it for other risk-taking activities. The devices also may be beneficial to other drivers or in certain driving conditions.

Does talking on a cell phone while driving increase your risk of a crash? The popular belief is that it does—a recent *New York Times*/CBS News survey found that 80 percent

Saurabh Bhargava and Vikram S. Pathania, "Driving Under the (Cellular) Influence," *American Economic Journal: Economic Policy*, vol.5, August 2013. This article has been excerpted and some references have been omitted; the article in its entirety may be accessed at www.aeaweb.org. Copyright © 2013. Reproduced by permission.

of Americans believe that cell phone use should be banned. This belief is echoed by recent research. Over the last few years, more than 125 published studies have examined the impact of driver cell phone use on vehicular crashes. In an influential paper published in the *New England Journal of Medicine*, [researchers Donald] Redelmeier and [Robert J.] Tibshirani—henceforth, RT—concluded that cell phones increase the relative likelihood of a crash by a factor of 4.3. Laboratory and epidemiological studies have further compared the relative crash risk of phone use while driving to that produced by illicit levels of alcohol.

> *[Our findings] confirm that cell phone use does not result in a measurable increase in the crash rate.*

The Puzzle of Cell Phone Ownership and Crash Rates

If alcohol, however, is responsible for 40 percent of fatal and 7 percent of all crashes each year, as reported by the National Highway Traffic Safety Administration (NHTSA), then [the data] illustrates a puzzle. Cell phone ownership (i.e., cellular subscribers/population) has grown sharply since 1988, average use per subscriber has risen from 140 to 740 minutes a month since 1993, and surveys indicate that as many as 81 percent of cellular owners use their phones while driving—yet aggregate crash rates have fallen substantially over this period.

No study has yet provided causal evidence of the relationship between cell phone use and crashes in the field. In this paper, we adopt a unique approach, and novel data, to estimate the causal link between cellular use and the crash rate. Specifically, we exploit a natural experiment which arises from a feature characterizing a large share of cellular phone plans from 2002 to 2005—a discontinuity in the marginal price of a phone call at 9 PM on weekdays.

We first provide evidence that this discontinuity in prices drives a sharp increase in the likelihood of calling for drivers using a proprietary dataset of calls from a leading network provider. Our data are restricted to calls routed through multiple cell phone towers in a contiguous region just outside of a major California downtown area during an eleven day period in 2005. Given the mechanics of call routing and signal switching, the calls could have been placed only by callers in moving vehicles. While scaled for confidentiality, we estimate the data comprises 106,000 to 477,000 calls placed by moving callers within a region spanned by 300 to 400 cell phone towers. To our knowledge, our paper is the first in the literature to use a large call-level dataset directly from a US provider, and moreover, it is the first to feature call data from moving vehicles.

[Our finding] presents this distribution of cell phones calls by likely drivers across Mondays to Thursdays, Fridays, and weekend evenings. While the downward slopes reflect the pattern of traffic across evenings, driver call likelihood rises by 7.2 percent at the 9 PM threshold when prices transition from "peak" to "off peak." We find no comparable breaks in likelihood for neighboring hours or at 9 PM on weekends. We present additional evidence on cell phone calls (this time by drivers and nondrivers) and 30,000 pricing plans across 26 markets to affirm the sensitivity of cellular users to the 9 PM price threshold. The rise in call likelihood at 9 PM represents the first stage of our analysis.

No Change in Crash Rate at the 9 PM Threshold

We next test whether the rise in call likelihood at the threshold leads to a corresponding rise in the crash rate. In order to smooth crash counts that are subject to well recognized periodicity due to reporting conventions, we aggregate crashes into bins of varying sizes. While this strategy improves estimate precision, it introduces a bias due to potential covariate changes away from the threshold. To account for such movement in covariates, we adopt a double-difference approach to compare the change in crashes at the threshold to the analogous change in a control period prior to the prevalence of 9 PM pricing plans and characterized by low cellular use.

[Our finding] plots the universe of crashes for the state of California on Monday to Thursday evenings in 2005 and during the control period from 1995 to 1998. The plot, and subsequent regressions, indicate that crash rates in 2005, or in the extended time frame of 2002 to 2005, do not appear to change across the 9 PM threshold relative to the preperiod. We then generalize our crash analysis to include eight additional states for which we have the universe of crash data. Placebo tests of weekends and proximal hours, as well as robustness checks to account for the reporting bias in crashes, confirm that cell phone use does not result in a measurable increase in the crash rate.

Given the economic value of cell phone use to drivers, our paper casts doubt on at least some policies restricting driver cell phone usage.

Our estimates of the relative rise in crashes and call likelihood at 9 PM imply a 3.0 upper bound in the crash risk odds ratio (and a 1 s.e. upper bound of 1.4) under credible assumptions regarding evening cell phone use. This not only rejects the 4.3 fold increase in crash risk estimated by RT, but the confidence interval of our estimate fails to overlap with that of RT. The analysis further suggests that cellular use is not analogous to drunk driving as some policymakers and academics have averred. The upper bounds of this study easily rule out the crash risk of 7 associated with positive levels of blood alcohol and the crash risk of 13 associated with illegal limits of blood alcohol.

The Caveats of the Findings

Our finding is subject to caveats. First, we assess only the local average treatment effect of cell phone use across all drivers and driving conditions around 9 PM from Mondays to Thursdays. Comparisons to other studies, including RT, should be tempered by the recognition that different estimates may reflect distinct local treatment effects. While we observe no obvious threats to the external validity of the present study, such validity rests on complicated differences in traffic patterns, driver composition, and the mix of call type at night from the remainder of the day. Second, while the upper bounds of our study may reject prevalent estimates of the literature, they may still constitute an economically significant level of crash risk. In light of this, we document the substantive implications of our confidence interval for the cost-benefit calculations of policymakers. Finally, our research design does not distinguish between handheld and hands-free use. However, we note that hands-free use was quite uncommon during our estimation period and that laboratory research has generally not found differences in crash risk across these technologies.

We employ two additional empirical approaches that confirm our finding that cell phone use is not associated with higher crash rates. A first approach exploits the nonlinear and heterogeneous take up of cell phone technology across the smallest geographic regions for which data on cellular ownership is available. A second, related, approach estimates the impact of recent legislative bans on handheld cell phones on fatal crashes in a number of states and municipalities.

We offer three main explanations to reconcile our findings with existing research. One possibility is that drivers compensate for the dangers of cell phone use by driving more carefully. [Researchers Robert W.] Hahn and [Paul C.] Tetlock suggest a second explanation for the absence of an observable effect: drivers with some affinity for risk-taking may be substituting one source of risk (e.g., speaking with a passenger or listening to the radio) with another (i.e., cell phone use). A third possibility is that cell phones may be dangerous for some drivers or under particular driving conditions, but are beneficial for other drivers or under alternative driving conditions.

Policy Implications

Our findings have policy implications. Every state has considered some form of legislation to restrict the use of cell phones—or to require the use of hands-free devices—while driving for some or all groups of drivers, and 37 states already have such legislation on the books. Yet given the economic value of cell phone use to drivers, our paper casts doubt on at least some policies restricting driver cell phone usage. For instance, if current [drivers] compensate for their phone use with more careful driving, then there may be a rationale for penalizing cellular use as a secondary, but not as a primary, offense. If cellular use is the product of risk substitution, then any legislative ban is inefficient. And if there is heterogeneity in the effect across drivers and driving conditions, then partial and targeted bans are appropriated.

2

Children Distract Drivers as Much as Cell Phone Use

David Petrie

Based in Springfield, Massachusetts, David Petrie works for Channing Bette Company, an educational publishing firm.

The US Department of Transportation identifies texting as the most dangerous driver distraction, leading drivers to take their eyes off the road, hands off the wheel, and minds off the task of driving. Nonetheless, driving alone with an infant can be equally as distracting in all three ways—visually, manually, and cognitively—with disruptions such as crying, screaming, and throwing toys. In fact, driving with young children has been cited as a leading cause of crashes caused by distraction, but the campaign against distracted driving is limited to the use of cell phones. Instead, the message to deter cell phone use should be changed from putting down the devices to pulling over and stopping.

Experts at the United States Department of Transportation say there are three types of driver distractions:

- Visual distractions lead drivers to take their eyes off the road.

- Manual distractions lead drivers to take their hands off the wheel.

- Cognitive distractions lead drivers to take their minds off what they're doing.

According to these experts, texting is the most alarming driver activity because it involves all three types of distractions.

Have these experts ever driven in a car with an infant?

Driving with an Infant Can Be a Nightmare

Driving alone in a car with an infant can be a nightmare. Take my oldest. To keep our house peaceful, we made sure she was completely addicted to Binkies two hours out of the womb. Still, a five-point babyseat harness would send her into such a tizzy that even pacifiers stopped working. When I had to drive her somewhere alone, I'd strap her in to her car seat, then I'd start the car, and then she'd start to wail. I'd give her a pacifier and she'd chuck it onto the floor. I'd drive a quarter mile, stop, retrieve the pacifier, and then repeat the process.

How did I clean the Binky? On good days I had coffee in the car. On bad days . . . I'll save you from the details.

I quickly learned to drive with multiple pacifiers, so as soon as she'd chuck one I'd reach back and pop another one into her mouth. She'd take a few sucks from that pacifier, chuck it, start to scream, and I'd reach back with another one.

The U.S. Department of Transportation created a website to get people to stop texting while driving. Why haven't they created a website to stop people from driving with kids in the car?

While I drove and while my daughter chucked Binkies I dealt with all three types of driver distractions:

- Visual distractions took my eyes off the road as I tried to see where the pacifier landed.

- Manual distractions took my hands off the wheel as I reached behind my seat and fished around the floor.

- Cognitive distractions took my mind off of the road as I asked myself why-oh-why had I ever thought having a child was a good idea.

The Limited Campaign Against Distracted Driving

Distracted driving is a huge problem, but to limit a campaign to one source of distraction is unfortunate at best. One study showed that 60 percent of parents felt driving alone with an infant strapped in a rear-facing car seat in the back seat was "very distracting." Eighty percent feared it could cause an accident. In 2001 the American Automobile Association reported that young children in the car were one of the leading causes of driver-distraction crashes for people ages 20 to 29. Texting might be more widespread now, but the impact of a screaming child certainly hasn't changed.

The U.S. Department of Transportation created a website to get people to stop texting while driving. Why haven't they created a website to stop people from driving with kids in the car?

The fix to distracted driving hasn't changed. The Department of Transportation says, "The message is simple—Put it down!" I think they send the wrong message. People are putting their cell phones down—in their laps, so the police can't see them texting behind the wheel. Experts at the Institute for Highway Safety recently said this could increase the risk of accidents.

"Pull Over and Stop"

I think the message needs to be, "Pull over and stop."

When I'd finally lose patience with my daughter I'd pull over and get out. I'd lean against the back of my car, hazard lights flashing, and try to find some inner peace before climbing back behind the wheel. When I pulled over I presented zero risk for crashing. People would stop to ask if I needed help, but once they heard the screaming they'd simply nod and drive away. Out of gas? No problem. That noise? Good luck.

One day my wife discovered a ribbon that came with clips on either end. One clip snapped to the handle of the pacifier and the other end clipped to the car seat. When my daughter chucked the pacifier I only needed to reach back and find the ribbon before reeling in the pacifier like a fish. I felt safer, but the screaming still drove me nuts.

The clip and ribbon weren't perfect. There were times my little girl would chuck her Binky so hard that it would swing around like a tether ball and smack her in the eye. When that happened I suffered from a different driver distraction: laughter.

"You don't want that Binky?" I'd snicker to myself. "It looks like that Binky doesn't want you, either."

My kids are all a lot older now, but I still need to pull over at times. Sometimes I do it so quickly that the shock quiets them before we come to a complete stop. I then turn and remind them of two things: I want to drive safely so that they'll live long and healthy lives, and if they don't want to help me drive safely then they can find some other way to get around.

What do you think the message should be? "Put it down," "Pull over and stop," or something else?

3

Cell Phone Use While Driving Should Be Banned

Christopher A. Hart

Christopher A. Hart is vice chairman of the National Transportation Safety Board (NTSB), an independent federal agency that investigates transportation accidents and promotes transportation safety.

Highway fatalities have experienced a downward trend, but the growing number of accidents involving drivers distracted by cell phones and other portable electronic devices (PEDs) is a concern. One study reveals that when drivers talk, text, e-mail, or access the Internet on their cell phones, their likelihood of an accident increases by more than 163 times. Furthermore, other research indicates that talking on handheld and hands-free cell phones similarly degrade driving performance. To keep drivers focused on driving, a nationwide ban on the nonemergency use of these devices is recommended. A multipronged approach to supporting this ban with effective laws, high visibility enforcement, and educational campaigns can reduce driver distraction and improve road safety.

Good morning Chairman [Charles] Fuschillo and members of the Senate Committee on Transportation. Thank you for inviting the National Transportation Safety Board (NTSB) to Albany to discuss its recent recommendation on the use by drivers of cellular telephones (cell phones) and

Christopher A. Hart, "Testimony Before the Senate Committee on Transportation State of New York on NTSB Recommendation Addressing Distracted Driving Albany, New York," www.ntsb.gov, February 13, 2012.

other portable electronic devices (PED) while driving. This recommendation, issued this past December [in 2011], represents what we have learned over the last 10 years from multiple accident investigations involving PED distractions.

The NTSB is an independent Federal agency charged by Congress to investigate transportation accidents, determine the probable cause, and make recommendations to prevent a recurrence. The recommendations that arise from these investigations and safety studies are the NTSB's most important tool for bringing about life-saving changes.

> *The NTSB [recommends] that all 50 states and the District of Columbia ban the nonemergency use of all portable electronic devices . . . for all drivers.*

The NTSB is concerned about the growing number of highway crashes that involve driver distraction, particularly by PEDs. Despite the downward trend in highway fatalities, almost 33,000 people were killed on the nation's highways in 2010. National Highway Traffic Safety Administration (NHTSA) data for 2010 indicate that 3,092 deaths, about one in 10, occurred in a distraction-affected crash, and we are concerned that the increasing use by the general population of cell phones and PEDs will result in more cell phone and PED-related accidents and fatalities on our nation's highways in the future.

Epidemiological, driver simulator, and naturalistic studies all show that the risk of a crash is higher when the driver uses a PED, although the increased crash risk depends on how the PED is used. Moreover, the use of PEDs is skyrocketing. According to CTIA-The Wireless Association, ten years ago, approximately 40 percent of the U.S. population, or 120 million people, subscribed to wireless service. Today, there are more than 320 million wireless connections, or more than one for every man, woman, and child in the country.

Recognizing the need for drivers to focus on the driving task, in December 2011, the NTSB recommended that all 50 states and the District of Columbia ban the nonemergency use of all portable electronic devices (other than those designed to support the driving task) for all drivers.

NTSB Accident Investigations

This recommendation is the most recent of several recommendations the NTSB has issued over the years addressing distraction. Since 2002, the NTSB has investigated four highway accidents in which PEDs played a critical role.

On February 1, 2002, near Largo, Maryland, a Ford Explorer Sport veered off the left side of the roadway, crossed over a median, flipped over a guardrail, and landed on top of a Ford Windstar minivan. Subsequently, a Jeep Grand Cherokee ran into the minivan. Five people were killed and one person was injured. Through our investigation, the NTSB determined that the inexperienced driver of the Ford Explorer was distracted by the use of a handheld wireless telephone at the time of the accident. Based on this investigation, the NTSB asked states to prohibit the use of interactive wireless communication devices by young and novice drivers.

On November 14, 2004, an experienced motorcoach driver, distracted by talking on his hands-free cell phone, failed to notice both that low-clearance warning signs were posted and that the motorcoach he was following had changed lanes to a lane in which the clearance was sufficient. As a result, he failed to move to the center lane and struck the underside of an arched stone bridge on the George Washington Parkway in Alexandria, Virginia. Eleven of the 27 high school students on the bus were injured. In his post-accident interview, despite the numerous warnings and his knowledge of the route, the driver stated that he did not recall seeing the bridge until the accident occurred. As a result, the NTSB recommended that states ban the use of cell phones by commercial driver's license holders with a passenger-carrying or school bus endorsement.

On March 26, 2010, near Munfordville, Kentucky, a truck-tractor in combination with a trailer, went off the left side of an interstate highway, crossed the median, and collided with a 15-passenger van that was traveling in the opposite direction. Eleven people, including the truck driver, died. The NTSB determined that the truck driver failed to maintain control of his vehicle because he was distracted by using his cell phone. As a result, the NTSB expanded its previous recommendation from the 2004 Alexandria crash and asked states to ban the use of cell phones, handheld or hands-free, by all commercial motor vehicle drivers.

Distraction is unsafe. It takes the driver's attention away from the driving task.

On August 5, 2010, on a section of Interstate 44 in Gray Summit, Missouri, a pickup truck ran into the back of a truck-tractor that had slowed due to an active construction zone. The pickup truck, in turn, was struck from behind by two school buses. As a result, two people died and 38 people were injured. The pickup driver sent and received 11 text messages in the 11 minutes preceding the accident. The last text was received moments before the pickup struck the truck-tractor. The NTSB concluded that this ongoing texting conversation distracted the driver and contributed to the series of collisions.

The NTSB has also seen PED distractions in other transportation modes. Of tragic note is the 2-train collision near Chatsworth, California, on September 12, 2008. A commuter train engineer, who routinely used his cell phone for personal communications while on duty, missed a red signal while distracted by a texting conversation. That train collided head-on with a freight train, killing 25 and injuring over 100 people. On October 21, 2009, two airline pilots were out of radio communication with air traffic control for more than an hour because they were distracted by use of their personal laptops. They overflew their destination by more than 100 miles, only realizing their error when a flight attendant inquired about preparing for arrival. On July 7, 2010, in Philadelphia, Pennsylvania, a barge being towed by a tugboat ran over an amphibious "duck" boat in the Delaware River, killing two Hungarian tourists. The tugboat operator was distracted by his repeated use of a cell phone and laptop computer and failed to maintain a proper lookout.

Distraction is unsafe. It takes the driver's attention away from the driving task. It can occur on our highways, in the skies, on our rails, or in the water and pose a risk whether it is texting, handheld, or hands-free.

Research

Our recommendation is not based solely on accident investigations. Numerous studies conducted by different institutions (academic and government), both domestically and internationally, make the case that PEDs are dangerously distracting. Two studies examining crash data, one published in the *New England Journal of Medicine* in 1997 and one published in the *British Medical Journal* in 2005, identified as much as a 4-fold increase in crash risk when engaging in a cell phone conversation. More recently, in 2011, the Swedish National Road and Transport Research Institute reviewed studies examining distraction resulting from cell phone use and found longer reaction times with cell phone use regardless of whether it is handheld or handsfree. Likewise, reviews conducted by researchers at Monash University in 2007 and at the University of Calgary in 2008 concluded that performance was degraded using both handheld and hands-free cell phones. Naturalistic studies have indicated that reaching for a cell phone, headset, or earpiece also increases the risks. And, in a 2010 naturalistic study of distraction in commercial trucks and buses, the Virginia Tech Transportation Institute determined that texting, e-mailing, or accessing the Internet increases the likelihood of an accident by more than 163 times.

There is no doubt that the adoption of "PED-free" safe driving behavior will require a cultural shift.

When using a PED, drivers do not just experience a visual or manual distraction; they also suffer a cognitive distraction while conversing on the PED. The Alexandria motorcoach crash paints a clear picture that this cognitive distraction while conversing is not limited to hand-held use of cell phones and other PEDs, and research further supports this fact. In both the *New England Journal of Medicine* and the *British Medical Journal* studies, researchers found no difference in crash risk between handheld and hands-free conversation. Carnegie Mellon University researchers explored the cognitive issue by taking functional magnetic resonance imaging (fMRI) pictures while study participants drove on a simulator and listened to spoken sentences that they were asked to judge as true/false. Listening to sentences resulted in 37 percent decrease in the brain's parietal lobe activation associated with spatial processing, an area associated with driving.

While most people recognize that texting while driving is risky behavior, many underestimate the risks that phone conversations can pose to driving. Among other things, many people mistakenly believe that talking on a cell phone is equivalent to chatting with a passenger. In a 2008 University of Utah study, researchers determined that a cell phone conversation is more distracting than conversing with a passenger. By observing 48 pairs of friends in a driver simulator, researchers found that drivers conversing by cell phone showed a more pronounced tendency to shift from the center of the lane and were 4 times more likely to fail to complete the study task than drivers conversing with passengers. An analysis of the conversations indicated that passengers take an active role in supporting the driver by more frequently talking about surrounding traffic and mentioning cues such as exit signs.

Multi-Pronged Approach

There is no doubt that the adoption of "PED-free" safe driving behavior will require a cultural shift. If change is to happen—like the progress in highway safety with widespread use of seatbelts, increased use of child restraints, and curbing drunk and drugged driving—it will take time and commitment as well as a three-pronged approach: good laws, good education, and good enforcement.

Past safety campaigns have shown that laws aimed at changing behavior are much more likely to enjoy long-term success when combined with high visibility enforcement and public information campaigns. For example, before states required vehicle occupants to use seat belts, their use was only 14 percent. After states started passing seat-belt laws, belt use jumped to 59 percent in approximately 8 years. Today, with stronger seat belt laws, high visibility enforcement, and education campaigns, seat belt usage is approximately 85 percent. There have been similar results with other issues. Over the last 30 years this multi-pronged approach has changed the way drinking and driving is perceived. Education, legislation, and enforcement complement each other.

A 2010 demonstration program revealed that laws, enforcement, and education could change cell phone behavior. The National Highway Traffic Safety Administration initiated this program in two communities, Hartford, Connecticut, and Syracuse, New York, focusing on talking or texting using a handheld device. Handheld use dropped 56 percent in Hartford and 38 percent in Syracuse. Texting dropped 68 percent and 42 percent, respectively. Recognizing that highway safety requires a multi-pronged approach, the NTSB recommendation includes provisions for high visibility enforcement and education.

It's not just about the distracted drivers—it's about the safety of everyone else on the road.

Everyone on the Road Is at Risk

Distractions have existed for drivers ever since the first driver drove the first car. The NTSB is especially concerned about distractions from PED use, however, both because of our accident investigations and because of the increasing use of PEDs by the general population. With more and more drivers using PEDs instead of focusing on driving safely, everyone on the road is at risk.

The NTSB's mission is to improve safety by recommending measures to prevent crashes, reduce injuries, and save lives. These investigations suggest this means getting drivers to focus on driving safely, rather than engaging in a conversation or text message on a PED or cell phone. Distraction is not just about holding a device in a hand or glancing away from the road; it is also about mentally straying from the driving task—multitasking that leads to cognitive distraction. Because driving does not require 100 percent of a driver's attention 100 percent of the time, drivers may think multitasking is all right. But research studies, statistics, and tragic lives lost show this is not the case. Even a momentary distraction of a driver's attention from the driving task—such as reading a text message or talking on a wireless phone—can have catastrophic consequences.

New York demonstrated leadership when it became the first state to ban handheld cell phone use, and this state also prohibits drivers from texting. The NTSB believes a significant number of lives can be saved and injuries avoided if New York expands its law to include all nonemergency use of all PEDs. It is past time to face the fact that distracted driving is a serious safety risk. More to the point, it's not just about the distracted drivers—it's about the safety of everyone else on the road.

Thank you for your consideration of this important issue.

4

Texting While Driving Law Rarely Enforced

Andria Simmons

Andria Simmons is a reporter covering crime trends for the At-lanta Journal-Constitution *in Georgia.*

Texting behind the wheel puts lives in danger, but enforcement of laws against the activity remains low. In Georgia, where a texting while driving ban was enacted in 2010, records show fewer than fifty convictions a month in a two-year period, far below convictions for driving under the influence of alcohol. Authorities state that enforcing the law is difficult; officers must prove that drivers are actually texting, rather than dialing or talking on their cell phones, and most drivers put their phones away in the presence of police. Additionally, many Georgia drivers dismiss the penalty of the ban, which includes a $150 fine and one point on their driver's record. Enforcement is much easier in states where any handheld cell phone use is prohibited, not just a ban on texting.

Motorists who are texting while driving may be risking life and limb. But they're at a pretty low risk for getting caught, recent law enforcement statistics show.

In the two years after a ban on texting while driving in Georgia took effect on July 1, 2010, state records reveal that fewer than 50 people a month have been convicted of the offense, for a total of 1,281 convictions as of Sept. 17 [2012]. That's a small fraction of the 22,500 people convicted of driving under the influence of alcohol or drugs during the same time frame. The Department of Driver Services (DDS) only tracks convictions, not the number of citations issued, DDS spokeswoman Susan Sports said.

Difficult to Enforce

Many law enforcement officers say the law is difficult to enforce. State troopers have only issued an average of 11 citations a month since the law took effect.

Lt. Les Wilburn, assistant troop commander for the Georgia State Patrol, said troopers have to prove beyond a reasonable doubt that someone was texting at the wheel, and not merely dialing a number or talking. Most drivers simply stash their phone when a cop is in sight, he said.

A driver's eyes are off the road for an average of 4.6 seconds each time they send or receive a text.

"We're having the same obstacles we've had since the law came into effect," Wilburn said. "They're looking for us now, because they know it's against the law, and they don't do it while we're in a car sitting right next to them."

The penalty is also paltry enough that many drivers dismiss the risk. A violation results in a $150 fine and one point on a person's driving record.

Enforcement of the texting law has been minimal in most counties, state records show. A notable exception is in Gwinnett County, where 665 thumb-happy drivers were convicted—more than in all other Georgia counties combined.

By comparison, Cobb County has convicted 64 drivers, Fulton 43, Clayton 20 and DeKalb 16.

Gwinnett County Police spokesman Cpl. Edwin Ritter said officers diligently watch for distracted drivers during routine traffic patrols, but the department has not emphasized enforcing the texting while driving law.

"We enforce it just like we do any other law that's out there," Ritter said. "If it's observed, [officers] are going to do something about it."

Studies show drivers who are texting are 23 times more likely to crash. A driver's eyes are off the road for an average of 4.6 seconds each time they send or receive a text, according to the National Highway Traffic Safety Administration.

Last year, there were 3,840 crashes attributed to cell phone use/distracted driving in Georgia, according to the Governor's Office of Highway Safety. Nine were fatal and 955 resulted in serious injuries.

The Centers for Disease Control and Prevention classifies three types of distracted driving: visual (taking your eyes off the road), manual (taking your hands off the wheel) and cognitive (taking your mind off what you are doing). Texting is particularly dangerous because it combines all three types of distraction.

"Just Let People Know They Are Watching"

Georgia's law does not distinguish between a texting in a moving vehicle versus one that is stopped. Eldin Pita, 26, of Sugar Hill, was texting his father while stopped at a red light near the Mall of Georgia in July when a Gwinnett County Police motorcycle officer caught him red-handed.

Pita admitted his mistake and said he typically avoids texting in the car. A friend from New Jersey died several years ago in a wreck that occurred because the friend was looking down at his phone, he said.

"I think I do deserve [a ticket] if I was driving," Pita said. "But sitting at a red light? I don't know."

Mandi Sorohan worked hard in 2010 to convince state legislators to pass HB 23, a law banning both talking on a phone and texting while driving for motorists with a learner's permit under the age of 18. The law was named after her 18-year-old son, Caleb Sorohan, who crashed his car while texting and driving on Dec. 15, 2009 and died.

A separate law, SB 360, passed at the same time to ban texting while driving for all motorists no matter their age.

Mandi Sorohan is disappointed that so few officers are enforcing the two laws. Several have told her they don't stop people for texting while driving, she said.

"I feel like they should at least pull people over and remind people [not to text and drive]," Sorohan said. "They don't even have to give a ticket, just let people know they are watching."

A Better Law

Some states, such as Florida and South Carolina, have no restrictions on phone use for drivers. In states with similar laws, such as Kentucky and North Carolina, enforcement is about on par with Georgia.

New Jersey averages ten times as many tickets a month as Georgia had in two years.

However, other states like California, New Jersey, Nevada and New York have laws that ban any handheld cell phone use. Police say such laws are much easier to enforce, because anyone holding a phone can be cited and officers don't have to try to distinguish how a driver is using their phone.

"When they have it up to their ear, it's an obvious violation," said Senior Officer Anthony Rusterucci, of Voorhees Township in New Jersey. "And then when you pull them over and they say 'Oh, I had it on speaker phone,' that still doesn't make it right because the law says it's hands-free."

As a result, New Jersey averages ten times as many tickets a month as Georgia had in two years.

"Is it a better law?" Rusterucci said. "It's a stricter law."

Georgia lawmakers considered but ultimately rejected a ban on all handheld cell phone use while driving when they imposed the no-texting law in 2010, said State Sen. Jack Murphy, R-Cumming, who sponsored the bill in the Senate.

Murphy said lawmakers decided banning all cell phone use was going a step too far. He thinks the current law already makes some people think twice about texting and driving. Murphy also thinks billboards and commercials aimed at raising awareness of the dangers of distracted driving will improve motorists' compliance over time.

He pointed out that it takes time to change driver's attitudes, just as it did for drivers to embrace seatbelt and DUI laws.

"Now, if you pick up your phone and start to text and drive, do you think about Georgia's law?" Murphy asked rhetorically. "A lot of people do."

5

New Cell Phone Technology May Help Reduce Distracted Driving

Alyssa Carducci

Alyssa Carducci is a freelance writer residing in Tampa, Florida.

Bans against cell phone use and laws prohibiting texting while driving undermine civil liberties, ignore other activities that distract drivers, and do not impact the personal choice to use mobile devices responsibly. Nonetheless, readily available technologies can reduce the problem without the enactment of new bans or policies. For example, one smartphone technology prevents drivers from texting or emailing and automatically sends reply messages in response to incoming calls or messages. And for commercial drivers, software allows fleet operators and risk managers to oversee the cell phone use of employees while driving. Legislation and existing laws should allow—not stifle—innovations in technologies that reduce driver distraction involving cell phones.

Driving distractions caused by cell phone conversations and texting have prompted legislation restricting or banning the practices in 30 states and caused [former] U.S. Secretary of Transportation Roy LaHood to declare texting while driving a "menace to society." Even [talk show host] Oprah Winfrey has mounted an offensive against operating a vehicle while using a keypad.

Despite recognizing the risks involved with drivers' concentration being divided between the road and writing, civil libertarians have been outspoken about their concerns that laws banning or restricting operation of mobile devices while driving might threaten personal freedoms.

"Some of the concerns I've had regarding anti-cell phone or texting laws is that it ignores two things. First, it ignores the legion of other drivers who are driving while distracted due to something other than their cell phone," said Carl Gipson, director for Small Business, Technology, and Telecommunications studies at the Washington Policy Center.

"Second," Gipson continued, "these laws are often overhyped. The reality is that no matter how many laws or regulations are enacted, it comes down to personal choice. 'Do I knowingly act in an irresponsible way to the detriment of myself and others around me? Or do I act in a manner that is most likely to lead to the safety of myself and others?'"

New technologies already on the market might resolve the divisive issue without enacting new policies and laws perceived as eroding personal liberty. Software company ZoomSafer, for example, provides smartphone technologies that prevent texting or emailing while driving and sends auto-reply messages on a drivers behalf in response to incoming texts or emails.

We must ... make sure that existing laws on the books allow for innovations in this area.

"Legislation Worsens Behavior"

The U.S. Department of Transportation estimates 16 percent of all road fatalities are caused by distracted drivers, but it recognizes banning driver cell phone use only can happen at the state and local level. Hands-free technologies operated through automobile audio systems may mitigate the perils somewhat, but LaHood has requested further research to determine whether these technologies also present too much of a distraction. LaHood has sternly opposed carmakers' integration of social networking software in vehicle navigation systems, such as OnStar's Facebook feature.

On January 5, 2011, ZoomSafer unveiled a new, patent-pending software service, FleetSafer Vision, which will allow corporate fleet operators and risk managers to measure and manage employee use of mobile phones while driving, regardless of the type of phone used. ZoomSafer founder and CEO [chief executive officer] Matthew J. Howard says his company's software complements current legislation.

"We believe that education and legislation along with technology are part of an effective solution to impact the complex behavior associated with the use of cell phones while driving," Howard said. "Unfortunately the data to date has shown that legislation alone has been ineffective and may even make the behavior worse because drivers now try to hide the fact that they are using their phone."

Gipson agrees legislation isn't the only answer.

"We must also make sure that existing laws on the books allow for innovations in this area," he said. "There are many stories that list dozens of companies working to solve this problem from the free-market end, rather than the regulatory or statutory end. If the stick isn't working as well as it should to discourage bad behavior, let's use the carrot," Gipson said.

Rising Concern for Businesses

Howard says accidents and associated costs provide sufficient incentive for companies to consider a product such as Fleet-Safer Vision.

"There is a clear liability and risk associated with employee use of cell phones while driving in the scope of work," Howard said. "The U.S. courts have consistently defined scope of work very broadly—whether it's a company vehicle or personal vehicle, an employee or company-liable phone, and during [both] business and non-business hours.

"The research is clear that visual distractions caused by use of cell phone increases the likelihood of a crash or near-crash by as much as 23 times," he added. "Therefore, the financial incentive for a company is to protect their brand and their bottom line—the cost of a crash with injuries averages about $120,000, and there are many examples of multimillion-dollar lawsuits based on an enterprise's direct or vicarious liability associated with such a crash," he said.

Howard says businesses are only now beginning to realize the amount of liability inherent in employees' use of phones and other mobile devices while driving. "Less than 18 months ago, this was a side story in local papers, but with the popularity of the topic in the mainstream press—'distracted driving' was Webster's [Dictionary] word of the year—it has become a board-level issue" for many companies, he said.

"In 2011 it will definitely be part of the risk management strategy for companies across the United States as well as their conversations with commercial-lines insurance providers," he said. "Our Web traffic and pipeline of sales opportunities clearly show that there is a growing desire to better understand the issue, create a safe driving policy, and ultimately establish solutions and practices to ensure compliance and reduce risk," said Howard.

6

Monitor: Fatal Distraction

The Economist

The Economist is a weekly British-based publication focusing on international politics and business news.

Once regarded as a tool to reduce driving fatalities, mobile phones today are distracting motorists and causing carnage on the roads. While technologies are being developed to help keep drivers focused on driving, each has numerous drawbacks. For example, head-up displays show information on dashboard screens to keep drivers' eyes from wandering, yet some drivers may be tempted to view e-mails, calendars, or other distracting content. Applications in moving vehicles can also disable touch-screens or stop calls or data from being routed to devices, but this presents a problem to passengers who need to talk or view text messages. Until self-driving cars become an everyday part of life, there is no easy solution to mobile phone distraction.

Mobile phones: People who use their phones while driving are causing carnage on the roads. Can technology reduce phone-related accidents?

For motorists, mobile phones have been both a blessing and a curse. In 1995, when 34.5m [million] Americans carried them, fatalities from road-traffic accidents began to fall—in part because accident victims and witnesses could immediately phone for help, says Peter Loeb, an economist at Rutgers University in New Jersey. Sadly, the trend reversed four years later. By 1999 there were 97.8m Americans touting phones, and in some cases calling and even texting while behind the wheel. The fatalities from accidents caused by drivers using phones began to outweigh the number of lives saved by the ability to summon help quickly. At any given daylight moment in America today, roughly 170,000 drivers are reckoned to be texting and 660,000 are holding a phone to an ear. Of America's more than 35,000 annual road deaths, a quarter are now linked to phone use, according to the National Safety Council, an NGO [nongovernmental organization].

It is a similar story around the world. The slaughter on the roads is often more terrible in developing countries where people may be getting their first phone and their first car, says Etienne Krug, head of injury-prevention for the World Health Organisation (WHO). In India the deadliness of drivers using phones surpassed that of drunk-driving three years ago, says Harman Sidhu, head of ArriveSAFE, an Indian pressure group. Mobile-phone distraction, he reckons, accounts for nearly a fifth of the more than 230,000 annual fatalities which the WHO estimates now take place on India's roads.

Some worry ... that the temptation to put more information into head-up displays could lead to drivers reading e-mails, scanning calendar appointments and so forth.

Can Technology Help Keep Drivers Focused?

More than 140 countries prohibit drivers from holding a handset to their ear. Some 30 or so also forbid the use of hands-free headsets. Most modern cars come equipped with hands-free systems to make and receive calls. Yet many studies show a deeper problem is the extra cognitive workload a driver takes on when talking to another person on the telephone. Texting is even worse and is widely banned at the wheel; texters are even more likely to kill someone or die in an accident. How can technology help keep drivers focused on the road?

Caller information is already displayed on a dashboard screen by the hands-free systems in some cars. It can also be shown in the "head-up display" of vehicles which project information, such as the car's speed, so that it appears to float beyond the windscreen. This can be less distracting because the driver does not need to adjust visual focus when looking between the road and a screen, says Sachin Lawande, a technologist at Harman, an American company which makes audio equipment for homes and cars. Such displays can also respond to gestures, like a wave of the hand, to silence a call instead of looking down for a button.

Some worry, though, that the temptation to put more information into head-up displays could lead to drivers reading e-mails, scanning calendar appointments and so forth. Better, some say, to stick to voice commands. These can be used to operate a phone no matter where it is in the car, says Peter Mahoney of Nuance Communications, an American firm which makes voice-recognition software. However, in April [2013] a study funded by America's Department of Transportation found that speaking text messages could be as dangerous as typing them. (Nuance's software was not used in these tests.)

A number of companies think the best tactic is simply to disable drivers' phones. DriveScribe, an app for Android smartphones that is made by a company called Drive Power, sends out auto-replies that the driver is unavailable while a vehicle is in motion, and unblocks communications only when the vehicle stops. Mike Moen, the firm's boss, concedes that many drivers will not willingly give up access to their devices, but says some parents require their teenage children to install the app if they wish to drive. Cheaper car insurance might persuade more drivers to accept phone-disabling features.

Another app, TextLimit, disables the touchscreen on iPhone, Android and BlackBerry devices when the GPS [Global Positioning System] in the device determines that it is moving at a preselected speed, says David Meers of Mobile Life Solutions, the app's developer, based in Atlanta. Aegis Mobility, a Canadian firm, is pursuing an alternative approach that would operate both within the phone and within the network: telecoms operators would not route calls or data to devices on the move.

No Simple Technological Fix

But what happens if you are the passenger in a car, or on a train, and you want to talk and text? Phones in moving vehicles could be unlocked if users pass a short test, suggests Andrea Henry of Iowa's Department of Transportation, which is planning to supply teenage drivers with Aegis Mobility's apps. Alternatively, signals around the driver's seat could be scrambled by a dashboard-based jammer such as the SkyBloc, made by Trinity-Noble, an American firm. It works well but may also block passengers' phones, says Eyal Adi, head of the firm's office in Ra'anana, Israel. Non-government use of such kit is also illegal in many jurisdictions (though a Panamanian shipping firm bought about 100 units). It seems there is no simple technological fix—unless, that is, self-driving cars become widespread, freeing drivers to use devices unhindered, and improving road safety all round.

7

Cell Phones Endanger Teen Drivers

Nancy Mann Jackson

Nancy Mann Jackson is a writer based in Huntsville, Alabama.

The problem of driver distraction and cell phones has grown nationwide with the increase of mobile technology users. Almost 28 percent of all automobile crashes are now attributed to drivers who talk or text on cell phones while on the road. Teenagers, especially, are part of the problem, as they are inexperienced drivers and more likely to engage in these dangerous activities; 26 percent of sixteen- and seventeen-year-olds report texting and driving. In response to accidents and tragic deaths, some teens are taking action to prevent their peers from using cell phones and driving, such as forming a safe driving group and developing a mobile app to stop young drivers from replying to texts.

When Wil Craig tells his story, teens listen. In 2008, when he was an Indiana high school senior, Craig was riding in his girlfriend's car as she drove and texted at the same time. Distracted, she wrecked the car.

The driver had no serious injuries. But Craig suffered a collapsed lung, four broken ribs, and a traumatic brain injury. He spent eight weeks in a coma. After he learned to walk and talk again and eventually returned to school, Craig began sharing his story with other teenagers—so far more than 10,000—to help stop teen texting and driving.

Widespread Damage

There are many more people who need to hear Craig's message. Driver distraction has become a national problem, especially because cell phone use has increased. Look around the next time you're on the road (as a passenger, of course), and see how many drivers are talking or texting on their cell phones. That can lead them to take their focus off the road and cause serious, even fatal, accidents.

Nearly 28 percent of all vehicle crashes, or about 1.6 million each year, can be linked to talking on a cell phone or texting while driving, the National Safety Council estimates. The problem is especially dire for U.S. teens: Among those ages 16 and 17, some 26 percent have texted from behind the wheel. (And 43 percent of those in that age group admitted talking on a cell phone while driving, according to a Pew Internet & American Life Project study.)

As the risks of texting while driving have become more obvious, lawmakers across the country have begun to take notice—and to take action.

Why Cells and Driving Don't Mix

While there are many activities that can distract a driver, such as eating or adjusting the radio while driving, sending text messages may be the worst. "Texting is among the most dangerous activities for drivers because it involves taking your eyes and attention off the roadway," says Justin McNaull, director of state relations for AAA, formerly known as the American Automobile Association. "Even taking your eyes off the road for two seconds doubles your chances of being in a crash." Not convinced? Stats from a Federal Motor Carrier Safety Administration study tell the story:

- Compared with 16 other distracting activities, texting had the highest odds of causing a serious crash.

- Drivers who were texting were 23.2 times more likely to crash than those drivers who weren't texting.

- When texting, drivers took their eyes off the road for an average of 4.6 seconds.

Likewise, making phone calls, even with a hands-free headset, while driving is more dangerous than speaking to a passenger. That's because a passenger will pause in conversation when the driver needs to concentrate on the road. "Even in conversation, an adult passenger can appreciate when the driver is doing something more demanding, like merging onto the highway," McNaull says. "Someone on a cell phone doesn't know or appreciate what the driver's doing." Only 2 percent of people are able to safely multitask while driving, estimates David Strayer, a psychology professor at the University of Utah. He has studied the effects that cell phone use while driving has on the brain. Even though teens are more likely to try multitasking, they're part of that 98 percent who can't do it safely, Strayer says. Driving is a new skill for teens, so doing multiple things simultaneously takes more effort for them than for more experienced drivers.

What the Law Says

As the risks of texting while driving have become more obvious, lawmakers across the country have begun to take notice—and to take action.

- Currently, laws in 30 states and the District of Columbia make it illegal to text or send e-mail while driving.

- Eight states plus the District of Columbia completely ban the use of a handheld phone while driving.

- Thirty-one states have separate restrictions for teens, including bans on using phones while driving or texting while driving.

Some teens even use technology to help them avoid texting while driving.

The penalties for breaking those laws range from fines to jail time. On the federal level, texting while driving has been banned for interstate truck drivers, and Congress is considering several bills that would encourage all states to pass laws banning texting while driving.

An Ounce of Prevention

Whether calling or texting while driving is restricted by law, smart drivers are rethinking the use of phones behind the wheel. However, it can be tough to ditch the phone. "People have a real desire to be connected and have the immediate ability to keep in touch with friends and family," McNaull says. "Giving up texting and talking on the phone while driving is hard." To avoid the temptation, McNaull recommends simply turning off your phone and putting it away before getting behind the wheel. Talk to your parents, and let them know that if you don't respond to their phone calls or texts right away, it's because you're driving. Avoid calling or texting your friends if you know they're driving at the time.

Some teens even use technology to help them avoid texting while driving. Zach Veach is a 15-year-old who races cars for Andretti Autosport. He began speaking out after a teen who had been driving for only two months was killed while texting in an accident near his home in Ohio. To help other teens, Zach developed urTXT, an application for smart phones that sends an auto response to the sender of a text, letting the sender know that the recipient is driving and will respond later.

Safe Alternatives

Like Zach, many teens are finding ways they can make a difference. Nebraska teen Emily Reynolds says texting and driving was once a big problem among her friends. After her older sister, Cady, was killed in a crash at age 16, Emily's family started the C.A.R. Alliance for Safer Teen Driving (named for the initials of Cady Anne Reynolds). The group visits schools to share the dangers of distracted driving with those who are just beginning to drive.

Since the C.A.R. presentation at her school, Emily says, she's seen fewer and fewer classmates texting while driving. When she finds herself in a car with another teen who is texting, Emily, who's now 17, doesn't hesitate to speak up. "I will absolutely say something, and it is usually along the lines of, 'You really shouldn't do that while you drive. Would you like me to text someone for you?'" she says. "Offering to do it for them gives a good alternative, and it gets the point across." Zach goes even further. "The first time I see [other people] do it, I tell them that I don't want to lose my life and they don't know how dangerous texting and driving is," he says. "Most people tell me they do it all the time and nothing has happened. [If] they refuse [to stop], I turn their car off and take the keys until they agree to put the phone down." Extreme? Maybe. But separating driving from cell phone use is a way to make sure crashes such as the one that forever changed Wil Craig's life never happen again.

8

Adult Drivers Are as Likely as Teens to Be Distracted by Cell Phones

Mary Madden and Lee Rainie

Mary Madden is a senior researcher with the Pew Internet & American Life Project. Lee Rainie is director of the project.

A 2009 study shows that while driving, adults are more likely to text or talk on cell phones than teens. For example, 47 percent of adults who text say they have sent or read a message and drove at the same time, compared to 34 percent of sixteen- and seventeen-year-olds who text. In general, 27 percent of all adults and 26 percent of all teens texted while driving, according to the study. Moreover, 75 percent of adults who own cell phones have talked on their devices while driving, compared to 52 percent of teens who own cell phones. This means that 61 percent of all adults and 42 percent of all teens engaged in some form of cell phone use while driving.

Cell phones appeal to Americans for many reasons, starting with the benefits of constant connection to family and friends. In the era of smart phones, instant and ubiquitous access to information, news, and games on handheld devices also draws users into deeper engagement with their mobile devices. Cell phones have become so popular that the number of adults who own mobile phones has often outpaced the percentage of adults who are online. A new Pew Internet survey finds that 82% of American adults (those age 18 and older) now own cell phones, up from 65% when we took our first reading in late 2004. Some 58% of adults now send or receive text messages with their cell phones. By comparison, a September 2009 Pew Internet survey found that 75% of all American teens ages 12–17 own a cell phone, and 66% text.

Many of these cell owners take advantage of the technology by performing all kinds of tasks in all kinds of places, including in the car and while they are walking. At times, their cell use is distracting and dangerous because it takes place when their attention is best focused elsewhere. Studies at Virginia Tech and elsewhere show that drivers using phones are four times as likely to cause a crash as other drivers. According to research from the National Highway Traffic Safety Administration, in 2008 alone, there were 5,870 fatalities and an estimated 515,000 people were injured in police-reported crashes in which at least one form of driver distraction was reported.

In the general population this means that 27% of all American adults say they have texted while driving.

As a result, seven states and the District of Columbia now ban all handheld cell use while driving, 28 states ban all cell use by novice drivers, 18 states ban all cell use for bus drivers, and 28 states ban texting while driving. The Distracted Driving Prevention Act, introduced last fall [in 2009] by Sen. Jay Rockefeller (D-WV), would provide incentive grants to states that ban texting and handheld cell phone use for all drivers and would require a complete ban on cell phone use by drivers under the age of 18.

This report covers related findings from a recent Pew Internet survey.

Nearly Half of Texting Adults Say They Have Sent or Read a Text Message While Driving

Close to half (47%) of all adults who use text messaging say they have sent or read messages while behind the wheel. That compares to one in three (34%) texting teens ages 16–17 who said they had "texted while driving" in our September 2009 survey.

In the general population this means that 27% of all American adults say they have texted while driving.

Male texters are more likely to report texting at the wheel; 51% of men who use text messaging say they have sent or read messages while driving while 42% of women texters say the same.

Those in the Millennial generation (ages 18–33) are more likely than any other age group to report texting while driving. While 59% of texting Millennials say they have sent or read messages at the wheel, 50% of text-using Gen Xers (ages 34–45) and 29% of texting Baby Boomers (ages 46–64) report the same.

Three-Fourths of Cell-Owning Adults Say They Have Talked on a Cell Phone While Driving

Three in four cell phone-owning adults say they have talked on a mobile phone while driving. That compares to just half (52%) of cell-owning teens ages 16–17 who reported talking on a cell phone while driving in our 2009 survey.

In all, 61% of American adults say they have had conversations on a cell phone while behind the wheel.

Again, men are more likely than women to report this distraction; 78% of cell-owning men say they have talked while driving, compared with 72% of cell-owning women.

Eight in ten cell-using Millennials say they have talked on their mobile phones while driving. However, Gen X stands out as the group most likely to chat at the wheel when compared with older generations. While close to nine in ten (86%) Gen Xers who own cell phones talk while driving, just 73% of Boomer cell owners and 50% of those age 65 and older say they talk on their phones while at the wheel.

Parents are more likely than non-parents to say they have talked on a cell phone while driving; 82% of cell-owning parents report this, compared with 72% of non-parents.

Men are more likely than women to report being passengers of cell-distracted drivers.

Half of All Adults Say They Have Been in a Car When the Driver Was Sending or Reading Text Messages on Their Cell Phone

Half of all American adults (49%) say they have been passengers in cars with other texting drivers. The same proportion (48%) of all teens ages 12–17 said they had been in a car "when the driver was texting" in our 2009 survey.

Men and women are equally as likely to say they have been in a car when the driver was texting. However, non-white American adults are more likely than whites to say they have been passengers of texting drivers. While 56% of black adults and 58% of Hispanic adults say they have been passengers of texting drivers, 46% of white adults report the same.

The likelihood that someone will be a passenger of a texting driver decreases dramatically with age. While one in three (75%) Millennials say they have been passengers in a car with a texting driver, 59% of Gen Xers, 37% of Boomers and just 18% of adults age 65 and older say they have had that experience.

Parents are considerably more likely than non-parents to say they have been passengers of distracted drivers; 58% all parents say they have been passengers when the driver was texting, compared with 45% of non-parents.

Nearly Half of All Adults Say They Have Been Passengers in a Car with a Driver Who Used the Cell Phone in a Dangerous Way

While cell phones are most commonly used for talking and texting, there is a range of other potentially distracting behaviors—such web browsing, video watching, picture-taking and gaming—that can divert a driver's attention away from the road. In all, 44% of adults say they have been passengers in a car with a driver who used a cell phone in a way that put themselves or others in danger. About the same number of teens (40%) said they had been in a car when the driver used a cell phone in a dangerous way in the 2009 survey.

Men are more likely than women to report being passengers of cell-distracted drivers (48% vs. 40%).

Millennials and Gen X are about equally as likely to report being passengers of drivers who use the cell phone in a dangerous way (59% vs. 52%). However, both groups are considerably more likely than older generations to report this experience. Just 37% of Boomers say they have been passengers in a car while the driver used a cell phone in a dangerous way and only 21% of adults age 65 and older say they have had that experience.

Again, parents are more likely than non-parents to say they have been passengers of cell-distracted drivers (49% vs. 42%).

A Sixth of Cell Phone Owners Have Bumped into a Person or Object While Using Their Handhelds

Of the 82% of American adults who own cell phones, fully 17% say they have bumped into another person or an object because they were distracted by talking or texting on their mobile phones. That amounts to 14% of all American adults who have been so engrossed in talking, texting or otherwise using their cell phones that they bumped into something or someone.

Millennials who own cell phones are by far the most likely to have bumped into someone or something: 33% have done so, compared with 15% of cell owners in GenX, 8% of Baby Boomers who have handhelds, and 3% of those over age 65 who own cells.

The physically-distracted crowd is also slightly more urban and well-educated than others. Cell owners who live in cities are more likely than rural residents to bump into other people and things (20% vs. 13%). And cell owners with college degrees are more likely than those with high school diplomas to be looking at their screens when they should be looking at their surroundings (20% vs. 14%).

9

Texting and Driving Is More Risky than Driving Under the Influence

Michael Fumento

Michael Fumento is an attorney and journalist specializing in health, science, and safety.

Texting while driving is more deadly than driving under the influence of alcohol. Tests show that drivers' braking distances are much worse while texting than being legally drunk, and texting while driving is seventeen times more dangerous than talking on a cell phone. But more education about the dangers of texting while driving is unwarranted; what is needed is legal coercion. Laws against texting and driving are inconsistent throughout the states, and the penalties and enforcement is weak. And although enforcing these laws is presumed to be difficult, it can be achieved with low-tech equipment and officer surveillance. Without bans and stronger enforcement, drivers must use common sense and available technologies to refrain from texting and driving.

"Border collie jill surveying the view from atop the sand dune." Those were the last words of Malibu plastic surgeon Frank Ryan, best known for "reconstructing" reality TV star Heidi Montag. It's not quite up there with "Et tu, Brute?" Yet it seemed important enough for him to text it just before driving off a cliff in August 2010. Jill survived.

We don't know what the message was in a 2007 accident involving the sender and her four fellow New York high school cheerleaders. But it probably wasn't worth slamming head-on into a truck, killing them all. And the 2008 Chatsworth train collision, in which 25 people died and more than 100 were injured, was officially attributed to the engineer of the Metrolink commuter train being distracted by text messaging.

Unfortunately, laws intended to deal with the problem of texting while driving, a major topic at the Transportation Department's Distracted Driving Summit on Sept. 21 [2010], reflect vital misunderstandings about why a cellphone combined with a moving vehicle can be so deadly and how to deal with it.

We don't need text education. We need legal coercion.

More Dangerous than Driving and Swigging Jack Daniels

Texting while driving can be more dangerous than driving while swigging Jack Daniels, according to studies. In a 2009 survey, *Car and Driver* magazine tested two of its staffers under a variety of conditions. It found that on average, driving at 70 mph, one man braking suddenly while legally drunk (0.08 blood alcohol content) traveled 4 feet beyond his baseline performance. But reading an e-mail while driving sober, he traveled 36 feet beyond the baseline result and 70 feet while sending a text. In the worst case while texting, he traveled 319 feet before stopping.

Yet 66% of respondents to a 2007 Harris Interactive poll admitted they've texted while driving, even as 89% said it should be banned. And it's the youngest drivers, who already are in far more than their share of road accidents and deaths, who do it most, according to government and insurance industry reports.

There are no reliable studies regarding deaths associated with driving and texting. But consider that in 2002, when texting was still a novelty, cellphone usage killed an estimated 2,600 Americans, according to a study by the Harvard Center for Risk Analysis. Yet texting and driving is 17 times more dangerous than just talking on a phone, according to a 2009 Virginia Tech study. And we sent about 15 times the number of messages in 2009 as we did in 2005, according to one wireless industry report.

One possible explanation for why we can't seem to keep our paws off those tiny keyboards is that surveys show that a vast majority of American drivers believe themselves to be above average—and not just in Lake Wobegon. Hence the belief that we need to ban thee but not me.

Transportation Secretary Ray LaHood's idea of putting cigarette-pack type warning labels on cellphones is as worthless as it sounds. We don't need text education. We need legal coercion. Yet 20 states still don't ban texting and driving, and only eight plus the District of Colombia ban talking on handheld phones while driving. None ban hands-free phones.

Laws Alone Are Not Enough

However, the mere existence of laws alone is not enough. Almost twice as many Californians in a new Automobile Club of Southern California survey say they now use cellphones while driving than admitted to doing so before it became illegal 20 months ago. And texting laws in four states surveyed have done nothing to reduce reported collisions, according to figures released by an affiliate of the Insurance Institute for Highway Safety.

Why? Penalties are a joke and enforcement is essentially nonexistent. A first offense is merely a $20 fine in California, and $50 for subsequent violations. By contrast, a first DUI conviction in the state carries a jail sentence of four days to six months, a fine as high as $1,000, a six-month license suspension and more.

Enforcement efforts are virtually nonexistent because everyone thinks it's so difficult. Yet equipment that detects outgoing radiofrequency signals is neither new nor cost-prohibitive and no more invasive than traffic control cameras, radar or radar detector spotters. But even such low-tech "equipment" as human eyeballs can work. Results from two pilot programs released Tuesday by the Department of Transportation show that. During a yearlong test, using a combination of public service announcements and programs in which officers were specifically watching out for drivers using cellphones, hand-held cellphone use while driving dropped 56% in Hartford, Conn., and 38% in Syracuse, N.Y.; texting while driving declined 68% and 42%, respectively.

"The laws are simple to enforce," says Jennifer Smith, president of Focus Driven, patterned after the highly effective Mothers Against Drunk Driving.

Yet none of this will have any effect if we don't recognize that the specific cause of the distraction "isn't your hands or eyes but your head," as University of Illinois cognitive scientist Daniel Simons puts it. "Texting requires you to take your mind off the road." Indeed, hands-free phones may induce a fatally false sense of complacency "if you falsely believe that you will notice what's on the road while focusing attention on your phone or a keyboard," Simons adds. That's why studies repeatedly show hands-free phones to be just as dangerous as hand-helds.

But current state laws universally allow hands-free phones, except in a few places for certain categories such as teens and bus drivers. And yes, there are voice-to-text apps that allow verbal text messaging, which some promote as a safer alternative.

For now, all you can do is control your own conduct, including downloading software that automatically blocks outgoing messages while turning off alerts for incoming ones. No message is worth dying for.

10

Hands-Free Technology Can Keep Drivers Safe

Consumer Electronics Association

The Consumer Electronics Association (CEA) is a trade organization representing the consumer electronics industry.

As a form of hands-free technology, Bluetooth can reduce driver distraction by wirelessly connecting cell phones to nearby devices in vehicles. Bluetooth headsets and attachable speakerphones allow drivers to receive and make calls hands-free with ease of operation. Installed car kits and in-dash technology integrate Bluetooth into the vehicle itself, which has several advantages, such as muting the stereo during calls and providing caller ID in ways that keep the driver's eyes on the road. However, common sense and caution must be used with hands-free technology, and the consumer electronics industry endorses legislation that prioritizes driver safety and supports future innovations.

You've likely heard of Bluetooth, the wireless technology that allows cell phones, for example, to connect to other devices in close proximity. When used with headsets or hands-free car kits, this technology offers drivers a convenient and potentially safer way to manage cell conversations while driving. And not only is it more convenient, in some states and localities it may be your only option for talking while driving.

So how can you enjoy Bluetooth hands-free calling in your car? Here's a look at some options:

Headsets

Bluetooth headsets are a simple way to talk hands-free in your car. Generally, headsets offer excellent call quality and simple operation. Since they're physically attached to you, headsets go wherever you do and may be a good solution if you make multiple stops or are constantly in and out of your car. This gives them a unique advantage over other in-car hands-free solutions. Perhaps their biggest downside is that they are battery operated, and thus require you to remember to keep one more device charged.

Speakerphones

Like their name suggests, Bluetooth speakerphones employ built-in speakers and microphones to let you take your cell calls hands free. Relatively small, they usually attach to your car's sun visor like a garage door opener. Power is less of a concern, as most contain built-in rechargeable batteries and can also plug directly into your 12V lighter outlet for powering or charging. Most models feature only a few buttons, which keeps operating them simple. Some offer small screens for displaying caller ID and call status. Models with built-in FM transmitters give you the additional options of hearing your calls through your car stereo over an FM frequency.

Remember, there's no device that can substitute for common sense to keep you safe on the road.

Car Kits

Car kits are usually installed (hard-wired) into your vehicle, which offers several advantages. For starters, installed car kits offer an integrated look with no dangling power cords, speakers or microphones. Second, they are typically connected to the vehicle's power, which means you never have to worry about remembering to charge them. They're always—pardon the pun—on call. Another benefit, many car kits can be installed to mute your car's sound system when your phone rings or you initiate a call. Depending on how many incoming calls you get, this can be a huge convenience. Some models also speak caller ID, which lets you keep your eyes on the road while trying to figure out who's calling. Finally, more and more models can wirelessly stream your music from your Stereo Bluetooth-equipped portable music player to your car's audio system.

Portable Navigation Devices

There's good news if you're also in the market for a GPS [Global Positioning System] navigation device. Many portable navigation devices (PNDs) offer built-in Bluetooth hands-free connections for your cell phone. Like installed car kits, PNDs with built-in Bluetooth use either their built-in speakers or an FM transmitter to play your calls through your car stereo. This convergence translates into added convenience for you, as spoken navigation commands are muted while the phone is in use. Some models also support Stereo Bluetooth music streaming, letting you stream music wirelessly to your car stereo.

In-dash

The final and most integrated option for adding hands-free to your car is a Bluetooth-enabled in-dash stereo. Bluetooth-equipped car stereo "headunits" totally integrate your voice and music streaming from your phone to your car's speakers. Like car kits and PNDs, most units will mute or pause the music when you place or take a call. In-dash models' larger displays or video screens make it easier for you to see the phone number and call status. Custom installation means that in many cases you will be able to use your car's factory steering wheel buttons to operate your phone and audio system as well.

Whether you frequently take calls in the car, or if your state or locality mandates hands-free talking while driving, you'll definitely want to shop for a Bluetooth hands-free device for your car. Make sure your phone is Bluetooth-enabled in order to be able to make and receive calls using a hands-free device. Also keep in mind that if you wish to stream music from your phone or portable music player, both the phone/player and the Bluetooth hands-free device must support the Bluetooth Stereo (A2DP) standard or "profile." Remember, there's no device that can substitute for common sense to keep you safe on the road. Please use cell phones and hands-free devices with caution. . . .

Policy Approaches and Considerations

The consumer electronics industry is completely committed to the principle that safety is paramount and a driver's highest priority must be safe control of the vehicle at all times. CEA [Consumer Electronics Association] has supported state legislation imposing limits on the use of in-vehicle electronics to ensure driver safety. CEA also supports ongoing consumer awareness and education and has compiled a list of state laws for electronics use in cars.

> *Policy approaches should recognize that in-vehicle electronics can enhance driver safety by improving situational awareness and focus.*

Policy approaches to driver distraction must be driven by well-grounded science. Recent "real world" data is now allowing us to understand the true impact of all distractions, including in-vehicle electronics, on driver performance. "Naturalistic" studies conducted under actual driving conditions should be given greater consideration than studies used with simulators.

Policy considerations must take into account both the current state of technology and the likelihood of future innovations. Policies should be carefully calibrated so as not to inadvertently prohibit new technologies that could benefit drivers. For example, regulations should not prohibit voice-operated texting where the real concern is manual entry and operation of handheld devices.

Policy approaches should recognize that in-vehicle electronics can enhance driver safety by improving situational awareness and focus. A driver using a GPS navigation system is safer than a lost or disoriented driver. Likewise, in-vehicle entertainment systems keep children occupied who may otherwise demand the attention of the driver.

Policy approaches should focus on driver behavior and activities rather than specific technologies or products. Scientific research has demonstrated driver distraction can arise from a wide variety of sources—conversations with passengers, eating, consuming beverages, smoking, tending to children, and other such activities. However, unlike these longstanding distractions, mobile electronics can also provide clear benefits to drivers and passengers.

Recent naturalistic driving studies have confirmed that manual texting while driving significantly increases the risk of a crash. CEA supports a ban on the use of handheld devices for manual texting while driving.

Research has also shown that younger drivers typically do not have the skill set to perform secondary tasks while driving safely. Accordingly, CEA supports initiatives that restrict mobile phone use for novice drivers or drivers operating under a graduated drivers' license (GDL).

11

Hands-Free Technology Does Not Keep Drivers Safe

Robert Rosenberger

Robert Rosenberger is an assistant professor in the Philosophy, Science and Technology Program at Georgia Institute of Technology's School of Public Policy.

Encouraging hands-free texting and calling while driving to en-hance road safety must be challenged. Numerous studies demon-strate that both handheld and hands-free phone usage compro-mise driver performance in hazardous ways. One view is that the brain does not have the capacity to simultaneously engage in two cognitively demanding tasks. Another view is that the habits of driving—which require automatic responses—may be over-come by the much different habits of talking on a phone. Which-ever view is preferred, driver distraction is caused by phone con-versations, not the visual or manual distractions of a device. Nonetheless, there is a gap between policies and the dangers of hands-free technology, and automakers are in an "arms race" to integrate dashboards with such communications and Internet technologies.

A 16-second television advertisement for the Hyundai Veloster features the car pulling into the screen, stopping, and sitting motionless in the middle of the road, the driver apparently talking to himself. Two police officers approach, each on a motorcycle, and they stop on either side of the vehicle. After a moment, the two officers pull away without incident and an announcer explains, "There's lots of reasons to love Veloster's voice text messaging. Here's two." The point of the short television ad is to promote the hands-free text messaging system built into the Veloster's dashboard, a novel feature available in many new car models.

The claim implicit in these developments—and made almost directly in the Hyundai Veloster commercial—is: Even though texting with a handheld phone is understood to be so dangerous that it is increasingly outlawed across the globe, hands-free texting while driving is conversely so safe that it should be actively encouraged. In this Viewpoint, I challenge this line of thinking.

The problem with the assumption that hands-free phones should not be distracting to drivers is that a multitude of studies have demonstrated otherwise. A serious problem is now emerging as the automotive industry increasingly builds hands-free calling, texting, and even Facebooking into the dashboards of new cars.

The Science and Policy Context

Multiple countries across the globe have enacted laws against talking and texting on a handheld phone while behind the wheel (see http://www.cellular-news.com/car_bans). In the U.S., 39 states outlaw texting on a handheld phone while driving, and 10 states maintain laws against driving while talking on a handheld phone (http://www.distraction.gov/content/get-the-facts/state-laws.html). But only a very small minority of countries bans hands-free texting or hands-free phone conversation, and no states in the U.S. ban hands-free phone use for all drivers. The implied understanding in such laws—insofar as only handheld and not hands-free devices are banned—is that it must be the visual and manual interface with the device that causes the driver distraction. However, the preponderance of scientific evidence reveals both handheld and hands-free phone usage to be associated with the same precipitous drop in driving performance. These findings point to a different understanding of cellphone-related driving impairment than what is implied by the existing traffic laws: it is the conversation that is the source of the distraction. That is, to explain why the large preponderance of evidence shows both handheld and hands-free phones to impair drivers to the same degree, the answer must lie in the mental distraction that comes with talking and listening to someone on the phone.

When only handheld—and not hands-free—devices are subject to regulation, a message is inadvertently sent that hands-free phone usage while driving is safe.

Just how dangerous is talking on the phone while driving? Research on phone records and accident data indicates a fourfold increase in crash risk for drivers using a handheld or hands-free phone. Cellphone-induced driving impairment has even been compared to drunk driving. And it is not the case that simply any conversation causes this distraction; evidence is emerging that passenger conversations do not result in the same driving impairment as phone usage. This is because passengers appear to be more aware of driving conditions than are interlocutors on the other end of the phone. Passengers thus modulate conversation when driving conditions change, and even participate in the task of monitoring the road. As [researcher] Frank A. Drews and his colleagues explain, this difference in driving performance "stems in large part from the changes in the difference in the structure of cellphone and passenger conversation and the degree to which the conversing dyad shares attention."

The disagreement between the science and the policy over the issue of hands-free phones is exemplified by recent discord between the U.S. government bodies tasked with addressing threats to traffic safety. In December 2011, the National Transportation Safety Board (NTSB) released an official, though in no way binding, recommendation for a ban on all cellphone usage while driving—including hands-free devices. The response has been mixed. For example, while Secretary of Transportation Ray LaHood has made combating distracted driving a central project of his tenure, he has distanced himself from the NTSB's recommendation, claiming "The problem is not hands-free. . . . That is not the big problem in America." He adds, "Anybody that wants to join the chorus against distracted driving, welcome aboard. If other people want to work on hands-free, so be it."

On the one hand, I sympathize with the apparent pragmatism of LaHood's strategy. Undeniable legislative progress has been made by aggressively addressing the distraction of handheld phones, especially on the issue of texting while driving. And this progress has come largely without raising the ire of a public and a business community that can be resistant to the regulation of hands-free devices. On the other hand, there are problems with this strategy.

First, when only handheld—and not hands-free—devices are subject to regulation, a message is inadvertently sent that hands-free phone usage while driving is safe. But as I noted earlier, the research shows this to be untrue. Second, the gap between the policy and the science is quickly being filled by new hands-free modes of cellular and Internet communication while driving.

The Source of Cellphone-Induced Driving Impairment

Describing the mental distraction of cellphone usage is tricky, especially in the context of a larger discussion in which some participants only acknowledge the visual distraction caused by looking away from the road and the manual distraction of taking a hand off the steering wheel. There are two general ways in which the mental distraction of cellphones has been conceived: inherent cognitive limitations, and long-developed habits of perception.

While researchers agree that cellphone usage results in dangerous driver distraction, there is no explicit consensus explanation of driver distraction in the empirical literature. Still, it is possible to abstract a general theory from the terminology through which these data are often cast: cellphone-induced driver distraction results from a human's inherent cognitive limitations. That is, using a phone and driving a car are understood to be two different tasks, each requiring some of our brain's limited stock of cognitive resources. In this view, the explanation for why cellphone usage results in driving impairment is because the brain does not possess the resources necessary to safely perform these two cognitively demanding tasks at the same time. For example, [researcher] Tova Rosenbloom summarizes the findings in this way: "the results are in line with the theory of inherent limited capacity of human attention . . . which predicts that the attentional resources allocated to one task (talking) come at the expense of the other (driving)."

Despite a driver's intentions to drive safely, a dangerous level of distraction is caused by the phone conversation itself—not by the manual or visual interface with the device.

In my own work, I have suggested an alternative reading of the same data. Building on a philosophical tradition called phenomenology, which specializes in the deep description of human experience, I have developed an account of what it is like to use the phone and also what it is like to sit in the driver's seat and operate a vehicle. My contention is that users maintain strong habitual relationships with these technologies. For example, responsible driving requires a driver to have an almost automatic relationship with the car; if a driver must stop the car suddenly, she or he must stomp on the brake pedal at the moment the decision is made. A driver cannot first make the decision to brake, then recall that braking is something that involves pressing a pedal, and then press the brake. Safe driving demands that, through training, the driver has developed responses so automatic that she or he can instead actively focus on the road, on the mirrors, on the movements of other cars, on signs and lights, and such. The habits of the phone lead a user to focus on different things. The phone inclines a user to direct attention to the content of the conversation and to the presence of the person on the other end of the phone. The inclination is to become engrossed in conversation and to have the discussion stand forward within one's overall awareness. My suggestion is that the phone inclines a driver to become absorbed by the phone conversation through a pull much like that of a bad habit. Even if a driver intends to stay focused on the road while talking on the phone, the long-developed habits of the phone may slither in and draw attention toward the conversation.

Whether you prefer the cognitive scientists' explanation that inherent cognitive limitations are to blame for cellphone-related driving impairment, or the alternative suggestion that impairment results from long-developed habitual inclinations to get absorbed by phone conversation, the implications are the same: despite a driver's intentions to drive safely, a dangerous level of distraction is caused by the phone conversation itself—not by the manual or visual interface with the device.

Hands-Free Dashboard Technologies

The new developments enabling hands-free cellular communication while driving come in two forms. The first are newly emerging voice interface smartphone applications. These are programs that enable users—including drivers—to operate a number of a smartphone's functions through voice command.

These include placing a call, dictating text messages, and having incoming text messages read aloud by the computer. The most influential of these is the iPhone's Siri application that offers a discussion-style interface with many of the smartphone's features.

Despite the danger science has shown hands-free devices to pose to drivers, the integration of these technologies into dashboards has become a key area of competition for the automotive industry.

The second form of hands-free communication available to drivers is cellular phone and Internet systems built into a car's dashboard. These new features enable drivers to call and text through voice command. Additionally, the devices may be engaged through buttons and scrolling thumbwheels affixed to the steering wheel or dashboard console, and information may be displayed on screens incorporated into the dashboard. One example is Ford's Sync system, which enables drivers to place hands-free calls, listen to text messages translated into an audio format, and even to reply to texts by sending one of a number of preset responses, such as "Stuck in traffic," and "Can you give me a call?" In an effort to compete with this and other companies offering similar features, General Motors is working to modify its OnStar system to facilitate calls and texting, and also to provide drivers a hands-free method for reading and entering posts on Facebook.

In its 2012 guide to new cars, *Consumers Digest* begins its review of these new dashboard technologies with a brief mention of the NTSB recommendation for the nationwide ban on all in-cab electronics—a ban which, if enacted, would place prohibitions on many of the new technologies the article is about to celebrate. With regard to the ban, the author surmises that, "in any case, we expect that automakers and phone companies, will reject the idea as unworkable." This seems like

an understatement. Carroll Lachnit, an editor at Edmunds
.com, makes a sharper observation, "It's a little bit of an arms
race. . . . There is a sense among carmakers that if they don't
start presenting these kinds of vehicle systems, they will be left
in the dust."

With the development of dashboard-integrated cellular,
Internet, and dictation technologies as an exploding area of
innovation in the automotive industry, challenges and opportunities are afforded to engineers and computer scientists. But
how should these opportunities be pursued? In light of the
scientific findings on cellphone-induced driving impairment,
practitioners of computer science and engineering ought to
develop creative ways to mitigate the dangers of these technologies as they advance. These projects could include, for example, devising more sophisticated options for drivers to pre-
program different automated responses tailored to different
potential incoming calls, or crafting ways to alert callers that
the person on the other end of the phone conversation is behind the wheel.

Safety Is in the Hands of Drivers

Despite the danger science has shown hands-free devices to
pose to drivers, the integration of these technologies into
dashboards has become a key area of competition for the automotive industry. The Hyundai advertisement mentioned at
the beginning of this Viewpoint is just one example of the
way hands-free in-cab devices have become the centerpieces of
marketing campaigns. And with the failure of the law to move
on this issue, responsibility for the safety of pedestrians and
the roadways is left exclusively in the hands of drivers.

Using a hands-free cellphone while driving is still legal in
most countries, and it is easier than ever as hands-free devices
are added to dashboards. This implies it is safe to use a hands-
free phone while driving, and encourages you to do it. But it's
not, and you shouldn't.

Organizations to Contact

The editors have compiled the following list of organizations concerned with the issues debated in this book. The descriptions are derived from materials provided by the organizations. All have publications or information available for interested readers. The list was compiled on the date of publication of the present volume; the information provided here may change. Be aware that many organizations take several weeks or longer to respond to inquiries, so allow as much time as possible.

Alliance of Automobile Manufacturers
803 7th St. NW, Suite 300, Washington, DC   20001
(202) 326-5500
website: www.autoalliance.org

The Alliance of Automobile Manufacturers supports a ban on text messaging or talking using a handheld device while driving. The Alliance advocates an approach that addresses the issue while preserving opportunities to enhance safety. It publishes its articles on driver safety online at its website.

Consumer Electronics Association (CEA)
1919 S. Eads St., Arlington, VA   22202
(703) 907-7600 • fax: (703) 907-7675
e-mail: cea@CE.org
website: www.ce.org

The Consumer Electronics Association (CEA) consists of two thousand companies within the consumer technology industry. CEA's mission is to grow the consumer electronics industry. The association is an industry authority on market research and forecasts, consumer surveys, legislative and regulatory news, engineering standards, training resources, and more. CEA supports the development of hands-free technology to protect road safety and provides such information to consumers at its website.

CTIA—The Wireless Association

1400 16th St. NW, Suite 600, Washington, DC 20036
website: www.ctia.org

CTIA—The Wireless Association is an international nonprofit membership organization representing all sectors of the wireless communications industry, including cellular, personal communication services, and enhanced specialized mobile radio. Information on wireless safety and driving is available at its website.

Federal Communications Commission (FCC)

445 12th St. SW, Washington, DC 20554
(888) 225-5322 • fax: (866) 418-0232
e-mail: fccinfo@fcc.gov
website: www.fcc.gov

The Federal Communications Commission (FCC) is an independent United States government agency. It was established by the Communications Act of 1934 and regulates interstate and international communications by radio, television, wire, satellite, and cable. Articles and reports on distracted driving and cell phone use are available at its website.

FocusDriven

PO Box 45333, Omaha, NE 68145
(630) 775-2405
website: www.focusdriven.org

FocusDriven is a group that advocates for victims of crashes involving cell phone-distracted driving and families of such victims. It is dedicated to increasing public awareness of the dangers of driving while using a cell phone and promoting corresponding public policies, programs, and personal responsibility.

The Insurance Institute for Highway Safety (IIHS)

1005 N. Glebe Rd., Suite 800, Arlington, VA 22201
(703) 247-1500 • fax: (703) 247-1588
website: www.iihs.org

The Insurance Institute for Highway Safety (IIHS) is a non-profit research and communications organization funded by auto insurers. The IIHS tests and investigates ways to prevent motor vehicle crashes and works to reduce injuries in the crashes that still occur. It also publishes the traffic newsletter *Status Report*. A search of the Institute's website generates a variety of reports and press releases on the issue of distracted driving and cell phone use.

National Highway Traffic Safety Administration (NHTSA)
1200 New Jersey Ave. SE, West Building
Washington, DC   20590
(888) 327-4236
website: www.nhtsa.gov

The National Highway Traffic Safety Administration (NHTSA) has developed a multitiered approach to helping teen drivers become safer behind the wheel. These tiers include increasing seatbelt use, reducing teens' access to alcohol, and promoting three-stage graduated driver licensing. Articles and reports on distracted driving and driver performance can be accessed on the NHTSA website.

National Safety Council (NSC)
1121 Spring Lake Dr., Itasca, IL   60143-3201
(800) 621-7615 • fax: (630) 285-1315
e-mail: info@nsc.org
website: www.nsc.org

The National Safety Council (NSC) is dedicated to saving lives by preventing injuries and deaths at work, in homes and communities, and on the roads. NSC partners with businesses, elected officials, and the public to make an impact in areas such as distracted driving, teen driving, workplace safety, and safety in the home and community. The group's website provides information to both parents and teenagers about modifying risky behavior while driving.

Network of Employers for Traffic Safety (NETS)
344 Maple Ave. West, #357, Vienna, VA 22180
(703) 273-6005
e-mail: nets@trafficsafety.org
website: www.trafficsafety.org

The Network of Employers for Traffic Safety (NETS) is an employer-led public/private partnership seeking to improve the safety and health of employees and their families. The organization is committed to preventing traffic accidents that occur both on and off the job. NETS publishes a monthly electronic newsletter and makes articles on cell phone safety available online.

US Department of Transportation (DOT)
1200 New Jersey Ave. SE, Washington, DC 20590
(855) 368-4200
website: www.dot.gov

The US Department of Transportation (DOT) works to ensure a fast, safe, efficient, accessible, and convenient transportation system that meets vital national interests. DOT operates a website dedicated to information on distracted driving, www.distraction.gov. In addition, statistics on traffic accidents can be found at the website of the DOT's Bureau of Transportation Statistics: www.rita.dot.gov/bts.

Virginia Tech Transportation Institute (VTTI)
3500 Transportation Research Plaza, Blacksburg, VA 24061
(540) 231-1500 • fax: (540) 231-1555
website: www.vtti.vt.edu

The Virginia Tech Transportation Institute (VTTI) is a research center at Virginia Polytechnic Institute and State University (Virginia Tech). VTTI seeks to save lives, save time, and save money in the transportation field by developing and using state-of-the-art tools, techniques, and technologies. Its research is affecting significant change in transportation-related public policy on both state and national levels. VTTI publishes its reports online.

Bibliography

Books

Candida Castro	*Human Factors of Visual and Cognitive Performance in Driving.* Boca Raton, FL: CRC Press, 2009.
Steven D. Gacovino, Edward Lake, and Luke W. Russell	*Distracted Driving: The Multi-Tasking Myth.* Charleston, SC: CreateSpace, 2014.
Anne Louis Gittleman	*Zapped: Why Your Cell Phone Shouldn't Be Your Alarm Clock and 1,268 Ways to Outsmart the Hazards of Electronic Pollution.* New York: HarperCollins, 2010.
Catherine Lutz and Anne Lutz Fernandez	*Carjacked: The Culture of the Automobile and Its Effect on Our Lives.* New York: Palgrave Macmillan, 2010.
Michael A. Regan, John D. Lee, and Kristie L. Young	*Driver Distraction: Theory, Effects, and Mitigation.* Boca Raton, FL: CRC Press/Taylor & Francis Group, 2009.
Larry D. Rosen	*iDisorder: Understanding Our Obsession with Technology and Overcoming Its Hold on Us.* New York: Palgrave Macmillan, 2012.

US Government, Department of Transportation, Federal Motor Carrier Safety Administration, and National Highway Traffic Safety Administration	*Complete Guide to Distracted Driving: Cell Phones, Texting, Electronic Device Usage, Accidents, New Guidelines for Car Devices, Commercial Vehicle Operators, Laws and Programs.* Mount Laurel, NJ: Progressive Management, 2013.
Tom Vanderbilt	*Traffic: Why We Drive the Way We Do (and What it Says About Us).* New York: Alfred A. Knopf, 2008.

Periodicals and Internet Sources

Paul Atchley	"Calling in Cars: What Are the Benefits?" Car Talk, December 14, 2011. www.cartalk.com.
Michael Austin	"Texting While Driving: How Dangerous Is It?" *Car and Driver*, June 2009.
Bruce Bower	"Cell Phone Distraction While Driving Is a Two-Way Street," *ScienceNews*, February 16, 2010. www.sciencenews.org.
Sam Grobart	"High-Tech Devices Help Drivers Put Down Phone," *New York Times*, November 21, 2009.
Jeff Hecht	"Hands on the Wheel, Mind on the Road—Not Cyberspace," *New Scientist*, July 22, 2013.

Insurance Journal   "Cell Phone, Other Distractions
                      Greater Threat to Teen Drivers,"
                      January 3, 2014. www
                      .insurancejournal.com.

Sarah Mahoney   "The Most Dangerous Drivers,"
                    Parents, March 2011.

National   "Cellular Phone Use and Texting
Conference of   While Driving Laws," April 1, 2014.
State Legislatures www.ncsl.org.

Deborah Netburn   "Can't Stop Texting and Driving?
                    These Apps Can Help," *Los Angeles
                    Times*, November 8, 2012.

Jane Shin Park   "The Real Risks of Texting and
                    Driving," *Teen Vogue*, May 2013.

ScienceDaily   "Hands-Free Talking and Texting Are
                    Unsafe for Drivers, Study Shows,"
                    June 12, 2013. www.sciencedaily.com.

Kevin Short   "Hands-Free Infotainment Isn't the
                    Solution to Distracted Driving,"
                    Huffington Post, August 8, 2013.
                    www.huffingtonpost.com.

Daniella Silva   "Distracted Driving: Safety Advocates
                    Call for Culture Shift as More US
                    Drivers Admit to Deadly Habit,"
                    NBC News, November 27, 2013.
                    www.nbcnews.com.

Maanvi Singh   "When Teen Drivers Multitask,
                    They're Even Worse Than Adults,"
                    Shots, January 1, 2014.
                    www.npr.org/blogs/health.

Debbie Swanson   "Can Technology Prevent Teen
                  Distracted Driving?" Edmunds,
                  October 10, 2013.
                  www.edmunds.com.

Index

Harvard Center for Risk Analysis, 54

Henry, Andrea, 41

Howard, Matthew J., 36–37

Hyundai Veloster, 62–63, 69

I

In-dash systems, 59–60

Infants and driving, 17–18

Insurance Institute for Highway Safety, 55

Iowa's Department of Transportation, 41

IPhone's Siri application, 68

J

Jackson, Nancy Mann, 42–46

L

Lachnit, Carroll, 69

LaHood, Roy, 34, 36, 55, 65

Lawande, Sachin, 40

Loeb, Peter, 38

M

Mahoney, Peter, 40

McNaull, Justin, 43–44, 55

Meers, David, 41

Metrolink commuter train accident, 54

Millennial generation, 49–52

Mobile Life Solutions, 41

Moen, Mike, 40

Monash University, 24

Mothers Against Drunk Driving, 56

N

National Highway Traffic Safety Administration (NHTSA)

demonstration programs by, 26

driver deaths data, 21, 48

introduction, 7–8, 11

texting and driving, 31

National Safety Council, 39, 43

National Transportation Safety Board (NTSB), 20–24, 27–28, 64–65

Naturalistic driving studies, 61

New England Journal of Medicine (magazine), 11, 24, 25

Neyfakh, Leon, 8–9

Nuance Communications, 40

O

O'Connor, Stephen, 9

OnStar system, 68

P

Pathania, Vikram S., 10–15

Petrie, David, 16–19

Pew Research Internet Project, 7

Phenomenology tradition, 66

Pita, Eldin, 31

Portable electronic devices (PED)

distraction from, 21, 23, 25

risks from, 27–28

Portable navigation devices (PNDs), 59

Pulling over, 18–19

R

Redelmeier, Donald, 11

Reynolds, Emily, 46

Ritter, Edwin, 31